A Year of Fun
JUST for BABIES

By Theodosia Sideropoulos Spewock

Fun seasonal activities, songs,
poems, and fingerplays—
plus practical advice
for parents

Illustrated by
Susan Dahlman

Totline PUBLICATIONS

Warren Publishing House
A Division of Frank Schaffer Publications, Inc.
Torrance, California

Introduction

Congratulations, new parents! You and your baby are about to embark on an exciting adventure together. The next four or five years of your child's life are very important because 50 percent of a child's intellectual development takes place between birth and 4 years of age.

You are your baby's first teacher. Your child will be learning very quickly during the early years and this is the foundation for later learning. Each day, spend time talking, smiling, touching, and cuddling with your baby. Your baby will like to hear you talk and to know that you are near.

Just for Babies has been designed to give you fun activities and helpful hints that cover the high points of development in your child's life from birth to 12 months of age. In this book you will find fun and practical suggestions for ways you can help your baby learn during each month of life, as well as songs and poems to enjoy together.

Lists of typical month-by-month development are provided at the end of the book. As you look over the lists each month, remember that every child grows and learns in his or her own way and at his or her own pace. Do not be alarmed if your baby doesn't exhibit every behavior in every list. If you do have questions or concerns about the development of your baby, your pediatrician can give you guidance.

Have fun growing, loving, and learning together!

Books

Baby will like to look at and listen to stories about things such as toys, babies, baby animals, colors, nursery rhymes, etc. Books that are durable enough for infants to play with have pages made of cardboard, vinyl, cloth, or textured materials. This is only a partial list. There are many more books available for you and your child. Ask the librarian of your local library for suggestions.

Books for Parents

Active Learning for Infants, Debby Cryer, Thelma Harms, and Beth Bourland. Addison-Wesley, 1987.

Baby and Child A to Z Medical Handbook, Dr. Miriam Stoppard. First Baby Press, 1992.

The Baby Book, William Sears, M.D. and Martha Sears, R.N. Little, Brown, 1993.

Baby Eats, Lois Smith. Berkley Books, 1994.

Baby Games, Elaine Martin. Running Press, 1988.

Beyond Peek-A-Boo and Pat-A-Cake: Activities for Baby's First Year, Evelyn Moats Munger and Susan Jane Bowdon. Follett Publishing, 1980.

Caring for Your Baby and Young Children: Birth to Age 5, Steven Shelov, M.D. and Robert Hannemann, M.D. Bantam Books, 1993.

Dr. Spock's Baby and Child Care, Benjamin Spock, M.D. and Michael Rothenberg, M.D. Pocket Books, 1992.

The First Three Years of Life, Burton L. White. Simon & Schuster, 1993.

The First Twelve Months of Life, Frank Caplan. Bantam Books, 1978.

Games to Play With Babies, Jackie Silberg. Gryphon House, 1994.

The Gift of Fatherhood, Dr. Aaron Hass. Simon & Schuster, 1994.

The Infant & Toddler Handbook, Kathryn Castle. Humanics Limited, 1983.

Infants and Mothers, T. Berry Brazelton, M.D. Dell Publishing, 1983.

Mr. Rogers Talks With Parents, Fred Rogers and Berry Head. Barnes and Noble, 1994.

Piggyback Songs for Infants & Toddlers, Jean Warren, Illus. by Marion Hopping Ekberg. Warren Publishing House, 1985.

Play and Learn, Carolyn Chubet. Longmeadow Press, 1988.

What to Expect the First Year, Arlene Eisenberg, Heidi Murkoff, and Sandee Hathaway. Workman Publishing, 1989.

The Working Parents Help Book, Susan Crites Price and Tom Price. Peterson's, 1994.

Your Child at Play: Birth to One Year, Marilyn Segal and Don Adcock. New Market Press, 1985.

Books for Babies

Baby Farm Animals, Illus. by Lucinda McQueen. Grosset & Dunlap, 1988.

Baby Inside, Baby Outside, Baby's Clothes, Baby's Neighborhood, Baby's Playtime, Baby's Toys, Daddy and Me, Mommy and Me, Super Chubby Books, Simon & Schuster, 1994.

Clifford's Animal Sounds, Clifford Counts Bubbles, Clifford's Peekaboo, Norman Bridwell. Scholastic, 1991.

Dinnertime, I'm A Baby Too!, Playtime, Quack, Quack!, Claire Henley. Grosset & Dunlap, 1994.

Colors, Jan Pienkowski. Simon & Schuster, 1987.

Happy Babies, Wendy Lewison, Illus. by Jan Palmer. Western Publishing, 1994.

Hey Diddle, Diddle, James Marshall. Farrar Straus Giroux, 1994.

I Love You, Sun, I Love You, Moon, Karen Pandell, Illus. by Tomie de Paola. G. P. Putnam's Sons, 1994.

I See You! A Little Mirror Book, Illus. by Carol Nicklaus. Random House/CTW, 1994.

Let's Eat, Let's Grow a Garden, Let's Play, Mother Goose, Sleepytime, Gyo Fujikawa. Grosset & Dunlap, 1981, 1982.

Let's Go to the Doctor, Photography by Elizabeth Hathon. Grosset & Dunlap, 1994.

Mother Goose, Tomie de Paola. G. P. Putnam's Sons, 1988.

Pat the Bunny, Edith Kunhardt. Western Publishing, 1984.

The Poky Little Puppy, a Golden Cozy Book. Western Publishing, 1994.

Zoo Babies, Zoo Colors, Zoo Doings, Photographs by Zoological Society of San Diego. Simon & Schuster, 1994.

The Newborn

Eye Catcher

Use sheets with bright colors and bold patterns in the crib or bassinet to stimulate baby's vision.

Happy Times

Feeding time should be an enjoyable and relaxing experience for you and baby. Spend this time cuddling, singing, and talking to your child.

Shake and Rattle

Shake a rattle or jingle a bell near one side of baby's head. Then shake or jingle it on the other side. Eventually, baby will search for the sound with his or her eyes. (You may also use a ticking clock for this activity.)

Look at This

Place black-and-white patterned designs along the sides of the crib for baby to see. Rearrange or replace them with different designs every two or three days. (See examples of some patterns on the page below.)

Sweet Melody

Hang a wind chime above baby's crib. He or she will enjoy listening to the melodious sounds it makes as you gently move the chime.

Which Cry?

Pay attention to your baby's crying. You will soon notice two or three types of cries coming from baby. One could be to signal hunger, one could be to signal some kind of pain (gas pain, for example), and another could just mean baby needs to be held.

In a Heartbeat

Hold baby on your left side. Baby will be comforted by the sound of your heartbeat.

Soothing Baby

A newborn's primary concern is adjusting to life outside the womb. Remember, baby has come from a place where his or her every need has been anticipated and taken care of. Baby is seeking comfort from his or her social interactions. Gentle voices and sounds will soothe baby, as well as soft stroking or caressing, which may simulate the feeling of the fluid that surrounded baby in the womb.

Start Early

Tell baby stories on a regular basis. Baby will not understand what you are saying, but he or she will sense the warmth of your touch and the comforting tone of your voice.

On the Move

Hold baby on your shoulder as you move around the room. Take a moment to stand near something interesting for baby to look at.

Music to the Ears

Place a radio or tape player near baby's crib. Play soothing music throughout the day.

Love and Trust

Spend many moments holding and rocking baby while singing a song. Softly whisper in his or her ear. These actions give baby a sense of love and trust.

Over-Stimulation

All new parents want to spend time interacting with baby, which is wonderful quality time for both parent and baby. Be aware, however, of over-stimulating baby. Actions such as yawning, arching the back, or sneezing may be signals from baby meaning he or she needs to rest calmly for

Colors and Patterns

Studies indicate that newborns are unable to see in color until sometime between the age of 3 to 5 months. Newborns can, however, distinguish between the brightness of colors. Bold colors and sharp dark-light contrasts attract their attention more quickly than pastel colors. Studies also show that newborns can differentiate between shapes and patterns.

Black-and-White Patterns

Black-and-white patterns are real eye-catchers for baby. Use white sheets of paper or posterboard and a black marker to create the designs shown below. Preserve each design by covering both sides with clear contact paper. Attach the designs to baby's crib at his or her eye-level.

Feeling Blue

Soon after giving birth, some mothers may feel depressed, have an uncontrollable urge to cry, be irritable, experience mood swings, or notice a change in appetite. Mothers may also experience fears of inadequacy as parents. Such feelings of distress are caused by hormonal changes in the body resulting from childbirth. Mothers who experience the "post-partum blues" can be reassured that these feelings gradually disappear. Talking to a physician or a friend who experienced this phase or calling a local chapter of Parents Anonymous can help ease the discomfort. There are also several helpful books on the subject. See the book list at the beginning of this book for some ideas.

Hush Little Baby

Hush, little baby, don't say a word.
Daddy's gonna buy you a mockingbird.
And if that mockingbird won't sing,
Daddy's gonna buy you a diamond ring.

And if that diamond ring turns brass,
Daddy's gonna buy you a looking glass.
And if that looking glass gets broke,
Daddy's gonna buy you a billy goat.

And if that billy goat won't pull,
Daddy's gonna buy you a cart and bull.
And if that cart and bull turn over,
Daddy's gonna buy you a dog named Rover.

And if that dog named Rover won't bark,
Daddy's gonna buy you a horse and cart.
And if that horse and cart fall down.
You'll still be the sweetest little baby in town.

Traditional

Baa, Baa, Black Sheep

Baa, baa, black sheep, have you any wool?
Yes, sir, yes, sir,
Three bags full.
One for my master, and one for my dame,
And one for the little boy who lives down the lane.
Baa, baa, black sheep, have you any wool?
Yes, sir, yes, sir,
Three bags full.

Traditional

The 1-Month-Old

Baby Listens
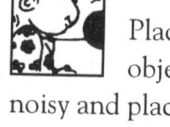
Talk and sing to baby while you engage in daily activities. Sing about what you are doing. At first, you will do all the talking. Soon, however, your baby will respond by waving arms and legs, cooing, babbling, and laughing.

Tummy Time
Place baby on his or her stomach. Select objects or toys that are colorful, bright, or noisy and place them around baby's field of vision. This encourages baby to practice lifting his or her head.

Diapering Corner
Hang several pictures on the wall near your diapering area. Baby will look at the pictures during diapering. Point to and name the pictures for baby. Change the pictures periodically so baby doesn't get bored.

Textures
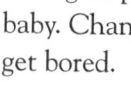
Gently stroke baby's head or body with materials of different textures. Use fabrics such as wool, satin, velvet, fur, silk, or terrycloth so baby feels textures that are rough, smooth, fuzzy, and bumpy. This will help develop baby's sense of touch. You can also introduce baby to things that are warm and cool.

A New View

Give baby a change of scenery by periodically moving the crib to different parts of the room.

Foot Fun

Securely fasten short pieces of yarn and a small bell to the end of an old booty or baby's sock. Use a permanent felt tip marker to add facial features to the puppet. Put the puppet on baby's foot and watch baby delight in hearing the bell while learning to coordinate hands, feet, and eyes. (Always supervise baby when using items having small pieces attached to them.)

Here and There

Play this game while baby is sitting in an infant seat. Ring a bell on one side of the seat. Then, ring it on the other side, while encouraging baby to turn his or her head toward the sound.

Human Touch
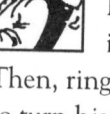
Use your hands to gently massage baby's body. Gently stroke baby's cheek with your fingertip. Name the body parts as you touch them. Sing the song "Here's Your Arm" on the page below.

Exercising

Slightly elevate baby's head with a folded hand towel. Place your fingers in baby's hands and gently pull his or her arms toward you. This exercise helps develop baby's grasp as well as neck and arm muscles.

Names

When you talk to baby, be sure to call him or her by name.

Rock and Read

Sit in a rocking chair and read nursery rhymes to baby. This can be a relaxing time for both of you. Baby will enjoy being cuddled and kissed.

Dancing Face
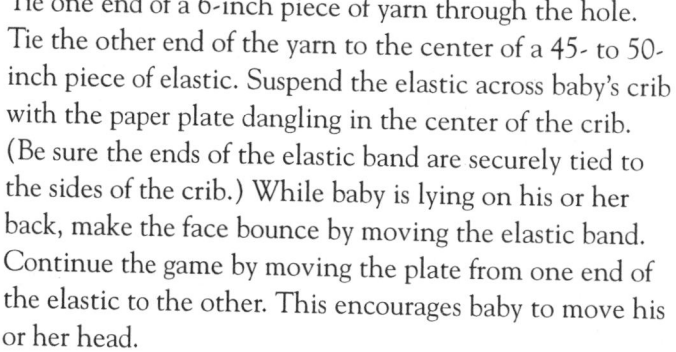
Draw a face on both sides of an 8-inch paper plate. Make a small hole at the top of the plate. Tie one end of a 6-inch piece of yarn through the hole. Tie the other end of the yarn to the center of a 45- to 50-inch piece of elastic. Suspend the elastic across baby's crib with the paper plate dangling in the center of the crib. (Be sure the ends of the elastic band are securely tied to the sides of the crib.) While baby is lying on his or her back, make the face bounce by moving the elastic band. Continue the game by moving the plate from one end of the elastic to the other. This encourages baby to move his or her head.

Toys and Playthings for 1- to 3-Month-Olds

- Mobiles
- Bright pictures of faces
- Rattles
- Large rings
- Toys for squeezing or sucking
- Vinyl or cardboard books with bright illustrations

Rock-A-Bye, Baby

Rock-a-bye, baby,

On the tree top.

When the wind blows,

The cradle will rock.

The wind rocks the cradle

To and fro,

Sometimes high

And sometimes low.

Adapted Traditional

Here's Your Arm

Sung to: *"Frere Jacques"*

Here's your arm, here's your arm,
  (Hold baby's arms.)

Watch it move, watch it move.

I wave it up and down.
  (Gently wave arms up and down.)

I wave it all around.
  (Gently move arms in circular motion.)

Watch it wave, watch it wave.

Here's your leg, here's your leg,
  (Hold baby's legs.)

Watch it move, watch it move.

I can move it up and down.
  (Gently bend and straighten legs.)

I can move it all around.
  (Gently move legs in circular motion.)

Watch it move, watch it move.

Jean Warren

Mama's Little Baby

Sung to: *"Mama's Little Baby"*

Mama's little baby a kiss can blow
  (Blow a kiss.)

And rub noses just like so.
  (Rub noses with baby.)

Two little hands can clap, clap, clap,
  (Clap baby's hands together.)

Ten little toes can tap, tap, tap.
  (Tap baby's toes.)

Karen L. Brown

Crying

All babies cry. Crying is the first form of communication that baby can use to express emotions and needs. After baby's first month of life, you will learn to distinguish between the length and intensity of baby's cries. These variations in crying may indicate baby's feelings of pain, discomfort, hunger, boredom, fear, fatigue, or a temperature change. Baby also uses crying as a way to release tension.

The 2-Month-Old

Echoes
Look into baby's eyes and imitate the sounds he or she makes. Don't be surprised if baby echoes your sounds.

Change of Scenery
Provide baby with opportunities to see and hear things from different perspectives. In addition to spending time in the crib, for a portion of the day place baby on a soft blanket on the floor. An infant seat is also ideal for moving baby around with you from one room of the house to another. Baby will be able to see family members at work or at play.

Keep Talking
While talking to baby, describe the things you do during the day. Baby will enjoy hearing your voice.

Batter Up
Place a broom handle or a narrow piece of wood across baby's crib. Fasten the ends of the wood to the crib. Tie one end of a piece of yarn onto a toy that makes a sound when shaken. Suspend the toy in the crib by tying the other end of the yarn around the broom handle. By batting at the toy, baby will begin to learn that his or her actions can create a sound. Replace the toy with another one to retain baby's interest.

Share a Magazine
Hold baby in your arms while you look through a magazine. Baby will focus on the pictures as you point to and describe them. He or she will also respond to the crinkling sound made by the pages.

Reflections
Place an unbreakable mirror in baby's crib or next to the diapering table. Baby will enjoy looking at his or her own face.

Shower With Love
Shower baby with hugs and kisses. Baby's trust and confidence grows with your displays of love.

Follow That Sound
Shake a rattle in front of baby's face. Slowly move the rattle across baby's field of vision, trying to keep his or her attention on the object.

Look at the Light
While baby is lying on his or her back, use a flashlight to slowly move light from one side of baby's head to the other. Encourage baby to follow the light with his or her eyes and head.

Peekaboo Puppet
Attach a small sticker to the end of a tongue depressor to make a puppet. If the sticker is wider than the tongue depressor, back it with a piece of paper and then trim the paper to fit. Play peekaboo with baby by raising and lowering the puppet. This activity helps baby focus on objects.

Whispers
Whisper baby's name near his or her right ear. Continue whispering until baby turns toward your voice. Then go near baby's left ear and keep whispering his or her name until baby turns toward your voice again.

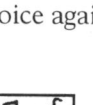
Soothing Tunes
Play music during rocking, feeding, and changing times to quiet and soothe baby.

Movin' and Groovin'
Gently move baby's arms and legs in circular or up-and-down motions in rhythm to the nursery rhymes you recite or to the songs you sing.

Crib Safety

In 1974, the U.S. Consumer Product Safety Commission established mandatory safety standards for the manufacture of cribs. If you or your babysitter are using a "hand-me-down" crib for baby and you are not sure if it was manufactured after 1974, check to see if it meets the following safety specifications:

- The space between crib slats is no wider than 2 ⅜ inches.
- The mattress fits snugly in the crib and tightly against the sides. Otherwise, baby's head can get caught in the space between a loose-fitting mattress and the crib.
- The crib is painted with lead-free paint.
- The crib has child-proof side locks to prevent side rails from accidentally lowering, causing baby to fall out of the crib.

Hey Diddle, Diddle

Hey diddle, diddle,
The cat and the fiddle,
The cow jumped over the moon.
The little dog laughed
To see such sport,
And the dish ran away
With the spoon.

Traditional

I Can Make a Baby Smile

I can make a baby smile
When I tickle her toes.
   (Tickle baby's toes.)
I can make a baby laugh
When I tickle her nose.
   (Tickle baby's nose.)

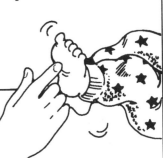

Betty Silkunas

Scrub-A-Dub-Dub

Sing this song to baby during bath time. Wash each body part as you sing about it.

Sung to: *"The Mulberry Bush"*

This is the way we scrub our hands,
Scrub our hands, scrub our hands.
This is the way we scrub our hands,
So early in the morning.

This is the way we scrub our head,
Scrub our head, scrub our head.
This is the way we scrub our head,
So early in the morning.

This is the way we scrub our elbows,
Scrub our elbows, scrub our elbows,
This is the way we scrub our elbows,
So early in the morning.

Continue verses using other body parts such as stomach, feet, ears, arms, legs, and so on.

Jean Warren

Safety Tips

- To minimize slipping, line baby's tub with a towel before filling it with water.
- Install a smoke detector in baby's room.
- When traveling, secure baby in a car seat.
- Do not warm baby's bottle in the microwave oven. The liquid becomes too hot very quickly.
- Avoid exposing baby to long periods in the sun. Baby's skin is very sensitive and can burn easily.
- Do not drink hot liquids when you are holding baby. They may accidentally spill and burn baby.
- Keep the side rails of the crib up when baby is in the crib.
- Keep small objects that baby can swallow out of his or her reach.
- Do not leave baby alone in a room with a young child or a pet. The child or pet may be jealous and try to harm baby.
- Avoid exposing baby to cigarette smoke.

The 3-Month-Old

Dancing to the Rhythm

Play music and dance to the rhythm while you are holding baby. Be sure to change your speed as you dance to songs with fast and slow tempos.

Finger Puppet

Place a white facial tissue or an old handkerchief over the tip of your index finger. Wrap a rubber band around the tissue or cloth at the first bend in your finger to form a head. Use a black felt tip marker to add facial features to the puppet. Use the puppet to talk to baby. Vary the tone of your voice.

Replay

Use a tape recorder to record the sounds made by baby. Play the tape for baby. He or she will "hold a conversation" with the voice by cooing, grunting, and repeating the sounds on the tape. Save the tape for your child to listen to when he or she gets older.

Carousel Mobile

Punch six evenly spaced holes around the rim of a sturdy paper plate. Cut out brightly colored pictures of faces and objects from magazines. Glue cardboard onto the backs of the pictures for strength. Punch a hole at the top of each picture. Tie one end of a 6-inch piece of yarn through each hole. Tie the other end through one of the holes in the plate's rim. Using a needle with a large eye, pass a 10-inch piece of yarn that has been knotted through the center of the plate. Use the unknotted end to tie and suspend the mobile from a dowel that has been securely fastened across baby's crib. Baby will enjoy making the carousel turn by batting at the objects.

The Outdoors

Take baby outside for a stroll. Describe for baby the things that he or she sees. If the weather is warm, place a blanket on the ground and let baby lie on it while he or she experiences the sights, sounds, and smells of the outdoors.

Rolling Ball

Roll a ball in front of baby while baby is lying on his or her tummy. Encourage baby to look at the moving ball.

Moving Melody

Sing a favorite song. Walk around baby and see if he or she can follow your voice. Sing louder if baby has difficulty in tracking your voice.

Textured Wrist Bands

Make several wrist bands for baby by cutting the cuffs off of old baby socks. Securely sew a different texture of fabric (fake fur, velvet, satin, corduroy, silk, etc.) around each band. Put a band around one of baby's wrists. Encourage baby to feel it. Describe for baby the texture that he or she feels.

Baby's Hand Puppet

Securely sew pieces of bright fabric onto a baby sock to resemble a face. Place the sock on baby's hand and encourage him or her to look at and touch it. (Be sure to supervise baby during this activity.)

Shake and Rattle

Place a rattle in baby's hand. Help him or her shake it to make a noise.

Beautiful Sounds

Hang a set of wind chimes outside. Encourage baby to look at the chimes as you move them to make them ring.

Lap Time

Hold baby in your lap as you read to him or her. This should be a pleasant and relaxed time for both of you.

Choosing Daycare for Baby

If you return to work after baby is born, you may need to consider daycare. There are several options from which you may choose.

- Family daycare: Care is usually provided for one to six children by an adult.
- Daycare center: Care is provided for many children by several adults.
- In-home care: Your baby is cared for by a responsible adult who comes to your home.

What to Look for in a Daycare

When selecting daycare facilities for baby, consider the following questions:

- Is the facility registered or licensed?
- Is the facility clean?
- Does the facility carry insurance to protect your child?
- What are the facilities' hours?
- Are the caregivers friendly, courteous, and gentle? Do caregivers appear to like children?
- Are you permitted to visit the center any time you wish to do so?
- Are special activities provided for children to promote learning?
- What is the facility's policy for taking care of children who are ill? Are children with contagious ailments kept in a separate area until they recover?
- Is outdoor play provided for children?
- Are there sufficient staff members to monitor and care for the children?
- Are the toys that are used by children clean and safe?
- Are the diaper changing areas clean and free of odors?
- What types of snacks and meals are served?
- Is the area child-proofed (free of dangling electrical cords, furniture with sharp edges, exposed electrical outlets, and objects that can be swallowed)?
- Is the staff trained to respond to emergency situations that affect the safety of your child?

The answers to these questions will help you decide on the most appropriate daycare facility for your baby.

Wee Willie Winkie

Wee Willie Winkie
Runs through the town,
Upstairs and downstairs
In his night gown,
Rapping at the window,
Crying through the lock,
"Are the children all in bed,
For it's past eight o'clock?"

Traditional

Baby is constantly listening and learning. Eventually, you and your baby will match sounds. This is the beginning of verbal communication.

Playpen Safety

You can help ensure that your wooden or mesh playpen is safe for baby by checking the following things.

- Mesh netting should have a weave that is smaller than the buttons on baby's clothing. This precaution helps stop baby's clothes from getting caught in the mesh, which may result in choking or strangulation.
- Be sure that the hinges on the playpen lock tightly. This helps prevent the playpen from collapsing.
- There should be no sharp edges on any part of the playpen.

This Is the Way Baby Rides

Sung to: *"The Mulberry Bush"*

This is the way baby rides,
Baby rides, baby rides.
This is the way baby rides,
Bouncy, bouncy, bouncy.

Bounce baby slowly on your knee while *singing*.

Jean Warren

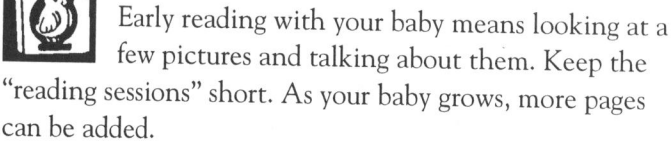

The 4-Month-Old

Window Gazing

Place baby in an infant seat. Position baby near the window and talk about the things you see outside. Point to the birds at the feeder, the snow, the rustling leaves in the wind, the rain hitting the window, the colorful flowers, the dog barking, the cars passing, and so on.

Cool Teething

Teething can cause discomfort for baby. Help relieve the distress by letting baby chew on teething rings that have been stored in the refrigerator. The cold sensation makes baby's gums feel much better.

Kick It

Suspend a rattle or a cradle gym above baby's feet. (You may also use an empty cereal box that you've partially filled with dry rice or beans and have securely taped shut.) Encourage your baby to kick the object. Give lots of praise for baby's success.

The Nose Knows

Help develop your child's sense of smell by letting baby sniff things such as tuna, colognes, flavorings and extracts used for baking, scented oils, vinegar, sauerkraut, and so on.

Bath Time Fun

Place a water toy, such as a small sponge, a plastic cup, or a floating object, in baby's bath water. Bath time will become play time as baby uses the objects to pour or splash water.

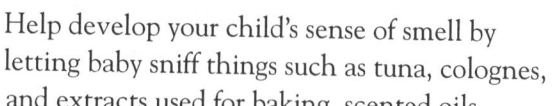

Fish Tank Fun

While visiting a pet store, hold baby in front of an aquarium. Point to the fish and describe what they are doing. In a few moments, baby will follow the fishes' movements with his or her eyes. If you have a fish tank at home, position baby in an infant seat so that he or she can observe the fish.

Early Reading

Early reading with your baby means looking at a few pictures and talking about them. Keep the "reading sessions" short. As your baby grows, more pages can be added.

Mirror Images

Stand with baby in front of a mirror. Point to baby's reflection. Then touch and name different parts of baby's body as you both look in the mirror. Move closer to the mirror and encourage baby to touch his or her reflection.

Get It

Sit at a table and hold baby on your lap. Place an object, such as a rattle, a cup, a plastic ring, or a toy, in front of baby. Encourage baby to reach for and grasp the object by saying, "Get the _____." Praise and hug baby for his or her accomplishments.

Sparkling Mobile

Cut four shapes out of the bottoms of old aluminum pie pans. Punch a hole in the top of each shape. Tie an 8-inch piece of yarn through the hole in each shape. Tie the other ends of yarn onto a hanger. Hang the mobile near the window. Baby will enjoy watching the sunlight reflected on the shapes. If it is warm outside, open the window and let the breeze move the shapes. Don't let baby handle the mobile, because the edges of the shapes are sharp.

Feel the Breeze

Use a straw or a toilet tissue tube to blow air onto different parts of baby's body. Baby will enjoy the sensation.

Wiggly Finger

Wiggle and slowly move your finger in front of baby. Encourage baby to grasp it. Give lots

Child-Proofing Your Home

As baby grows and becomes more active and mobile, extra caution must be taken to ensure your child's safety in the home. Make sure that:

- all electrical outlets are protected with covers
- medicine cabinets and cupboards containing cleaning solvents and other potential poisons are fastened with child-proof devices
- tablecloths that drape over tables are placed out of baby's reach so that they cannot be pulled
- small items or objects that can be swallowed are placed out of baby's reach
- sharp edges of furniture are cushioned or covered
- sharp objects such as knives, scissors, pins, and razors are kept away from baby
- pillows and toys are not left in the crib or play-pen (baby may step on them to climb over the crib or play area)
- baby's highchair has a locking tray, a wide base for stability, and safety straps that are not attached to the tray
- the water heater is set lower than 125°F to avoid scalding baby
- baby is never left alone near water (bathtub, sink, toilet)

Additional tips for child-proofing your home are outlined in Month 6 and Month 9.

Play

Plan several play periods with baby each day. Begin with short play periods and increase them as baby's attention increases.

Toys and Playthings for 4- to 6-Month-Olds

- cradle gym
- soft blocks
- mobiles
- unbreakable mirror
- jolly jumper
- rattles
- toys that make noise when shaken, squeezed, mouthed, and batted
- texture ball/toy
- water toys that float
- cloth books with bright, colorful pictures
- cloth doll
- busy box
- large pictures of faces
- toys for teething
- grip balls

Do not use balloons with babies or small children. Balloons can be easily broken and swallowed, which can result in suffocation.

To Market, to Market

To market, to market
To buy a fat pig.
Home again, home again,
Jiggety-jig.

To market, to market
To buy a fat hog.
Home again, home again,
Jiggety-jog.

Move baby up and down on your knee while singing or saying this rhyme.

Traditional

Pat a Cake

Pat a cake, pat a cake, baker's man.
Bake me a cake as fast as you can.
    (Hold baby's hands and do actions indicated.)
Roll it and pat it and mark it with a B,
And put it in the oven for Baby and me.

Adapted Traditional

The 5-Month-Old

Tug of War

Tie an elastic band around an empty spool. Hold the elastic end and dangle the spool within baby's reach. Encourage baby to grab the spool. Gently pull on the elastic to create some resistance on the spool. Baby will respond by pulling on the spool. Praise baby's efforts.

Where's Baby?

Hold a washcloth above baby's face and ask "Where's (baby's name)?" Quickly remove the washcloth and happily exclaim "There's (baby's name)!" Give baby a kiss. Repeat the activity as long as baby seems interested.

Open Space

Spend playtime with baby on a blanket on the floor. Baby will enjoy being in an unconfined area because there's more to see and experience! The crib and playpen can limit baby's exploration.

Puppet Talk

Make a hand puppet out of an old sock. Securely sew on yarn and felt scraps for facial features. Use the puppet to talk to baby. Change your voice to make it more interesting.

Bubbles, Bubbles

Use pillows or cushions to prop baby up into a sitting position. Blow bubbles in front of baby. (Avoid blowing bubbles in baby's face.) Encourage baby to reach out and bat at the bubbles.

So Nice to Meet You

Let your baby experience being around other babies. Observe how the infants react as they look, touch, and smile at each other. If one baby should begin to cry, don't be surprised if the others respond by crying, too!

Tickling Game

Tickle baby on different parts of the body. Say, "Now I'm going to tickle your tummy." Laugh along with baby. Kiss the body parts that you tickle.

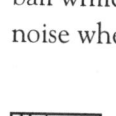

Floor Time Fun

While propped in a seated position or while on his or her tummy, encourage baby to hit a beach ball. Baby will delight in his or her efforts to make the ball move. You can also encourage baby to kick the beach ball while on his or her back. (A rolling toy that makes noise when it is pushed also works well for this activity.)

Texture Chart

Securely sew pieces of textured and smooth fabric onto an old towel. Attach the towel to the side of the crib so that baby can feel the textures. To help keep baby occupied during diapering, hang the cloth chart on the wall at the diapering area.

People Watching

Provide opportunities for baby to watch other children at play. Take a stroll to the playground and describe to baby what the children are doing.

Both Hands

Encourage baby to use both hands. Prop baby into a sitting position. Hold up a toy and tell baby to take it. After he or she has grasped it, hold it up again and encourage baby to use the other hand to get the toy.

Building Strength

With baby lying on his or her tummy on a carpeted floor, position the palms of your hands against the bottoms of baby's feet. Gently push against baby's feet. Baby will respond by pushing back. This is a great way to help baby strengthen leg muscles that will soon be used for crawling.

Clippety Clop

Sung to: "Row, Row, Row
    Your Boat"

Clip, clip, clippety clop,
Clippety, clippety, clop.
The old gray horse goes up and down
Until it's time to stop.

While singing, move baby up
and down on your knee or walk
in a circle with baby.

Additional verse: The old gray
horse goes round and round.

Jean Warren

This Little Piggy

This little piggy went to market.
    (Wiggle baby's big toe.)
This little piggy stayed home.
    (Wiggle baby's second toe.)
This little piggy had roast beef.
    (Wiggle baby's third toe.)
This little piggy had none.
    (Wiggle baby's fourth toe.)
And this little piggy cried, "Wee-wee-wee-wee,

I can't find my way back home!"
    (Wiggle baby's little toe.)

Traditional

**Your baby learns language from you.
The more you talk and sing to baby,
the easier it is for him or her to learn
to speak.**

Twinkle, Twinkle, Little Star

Twinkle, twinkle, little star.
How I wonder what you are.
Up above the world so high,
Like a diamond in the sky.
Twinkle, twinkle, little star,
How I wonder what you are.

Traditional

Dietary Tips

The nutritional needs of an infant differ from those of an adult. Your pediatrician can provide you with advice and dietary guidelines that will help you provide baby with the nutrients needed for proper growth and development. Use the following tips along with advice provided by your pediatrician.

- Sugar is linked to tooth decay. Therefore, only serve sugared foods and drinks in moderation.

- Avoid feeding your baby foods that contain artificial sweeteners (unless otherwise specified by your pediatrician).

- Avoid overfeeding baby. Do not force your child to finish every morsel or drop of food on the plate or in the bottle. Your baby knows when he or she has had enough.

- Avoid serving foods that are high in sodium or salt.

- Skim milk is not recommended for children before the age of 2. The fat content in whole milk provides baby with the calories needed to grow and develop.

- Because of possible choking hazards, never feed your baby foods such as peanut butter, peanuts, hard candy, hot dogs, grapes, blueberries, processed meats, popcorn, small pieces of apple, or other foods that are round, hard, or slick.

The 6-Month-Old

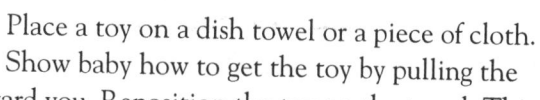

Let's Get It

Place a toy on a dish towel or a piece of cloth. Show baby how to get the toy by pulling the towel toward you. Reposition the toy on the towel. This time, encourage baby to retrieve the toy by pulling on the towel. Let baby play with the toy. Give lots of hugs and kisses for a job well done.

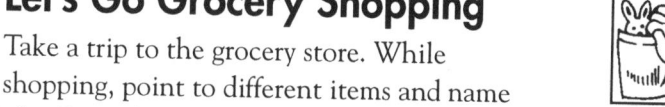

Let's Go Grocery Shopping

Take a trip to the grocery store. While shopping, point to different items and name them for baby. Describe their shapes, colors, and sizes. Talk to baby about the items you are placing in your cart. For example, "Mommy likes (food item). Let's get this for her." Here is (baby's name)'s favorite cereal. Let's buy a box for you." "We need some tomatoes for the spaghetti sauce. Let's pick a few." "Here is the food that our dog likes to eat. Won't he be happy?"

Spoon Puppet

Use permanent felt tip markers to turn a small wooden cooking spoon into a puppet. Draw a happy face on one side and a sad face on the other side. Baby will enjoy holding the spoon. You can make the puppet come alive by moving it up and down as it "talks" to baby.

Touch and Say

Put baby's hand on a part of your face or head (nose, mouth, hair, chin, ear, and so on) as you name it. Next, use baby's hand to touch the same part on his or her own head as you name each part. Continue the game by pointing to a different part of your head or face.

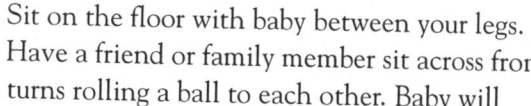

Back and Forth

Sit on the floor with baby between your legs. Have a friend or family member sit across from you. Take turns rolling a ball to each other. Baby will delight in watching the ball roll toward both of you and will enjoy helping you push the ball away.

Sounds All Around

When using household appliances, talk to baby about the sounds they make. Let baby see the appliances in action. Point out the sounds made by the electric mixer, washing machine, dishwasher, microwave oven, popcorn popper, kitchen timer, flushing toilet, door bell, radio, tape player, and vacuum cleaner.

Hide and Seek

Hide a small toy in one of your pockets, making sure that part of it is showing. Ask baby to find it. Allow baby to pull it out of your pocket and play with it for a moment. Then have baby watch as you hide the toy behind you. Ask baby to find the toy. Give lots of praise!

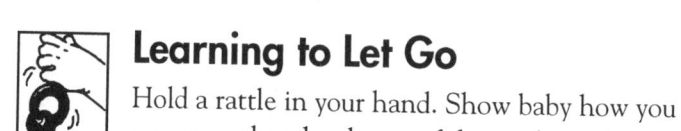

Watch Me Read

Let baby see you reading throughout the day. Besides having you read a story to him or her, baby can see you read a letter, the newspaper, or a magazine. Tell baby that you are reading, and why. Read aloud so that baby can hear your voice.

Learning to Let Go

Hold a rattle in your hand. Show baby how you open your hand to let go of the rattle so that it falls and makes a noise. Repeat several times. Place the rattle in baby's hand and encourage him or her to drop it by letting go. Praise baby for the noise he or she creates.

Familiar Faces

When a family member or other familiar person is in the room, ask baby, "Where is (name of person)?" Encourage baby to look around the room. Praise baby when he or she looks at the person.

Roll Away

Place a blanket on the floor. Position a toy at each corner of the blanket. Encourage baby to roll and reach for the toy.

I'm Hiding

I'm hiding, I'm hiding,
(Place small blanket over baby.)
And no one knows where,
For all they can see
Are my nose and my hair!

You found me, you found me,
(Remove blanket from baby.)
You figured out where!
Now you can see me
From here down to there!
(Point to baby's head and then feet.)

Adapted Traditional

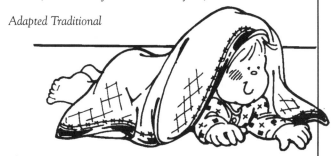

Baby learns through repetition.
When you're playing games, singing
songs, or reciting rhymes with baby,
repeat them over and over again.

Two Little Blackbirds

Sung to: *"Frere Jacques"*

Two little blackbirds
(Hold up two pointer fingers.)
Sitting on a hill,
(Make a hill with both hands.)
One named Jack,
(Hold up one pointer finger.)
One named Jill.
(Hold up other pointer finger.)

Two little blackbirds
(Hold up two pointer fingers.)
Flew away.
(Move both hands behind back.)
Jack flew back,
(Bring out one hand, pointer finger raised.)
Then came Jill.
(Bring out other hand, pointer finger raised.)

Adapted Traditional

More About Safety

The hazard potential in your home will be on the rise as your baby becomes more active. Very soon, your infant will be able to creep and crawl to all parts of the house. Therefore, it is extremely important that you continue to child-proof your home. See baby's perspective of your home by getting down on your hands and knees and crawling around the house. You'll be amazed to see things that have the potential of causing harm to your baby. Review the child-proofing procedures that have already been outlined in Month 4. Then refer to the following suggestions that will help you create a safer environment for your growing and active child.

- Assume that your child will put anything in his or her mouth. Therefore, keep potentially harmful things out of baby's reach.

- Adjust the crib mattress to the lowest point to prevent baby from falling out of the crib once he or she has learned to stand.

- Place safety gates at tops and bottoms of stairways.

- Check under beds and other furniture. Remove small, sharp, or dangerous objects that could choke or injure baby.

- Check low shelves for objects that could be pulled down and hit baby on the head.

- Remove items made of glass that are within baby's reach. Aside from cutting baby, broken glass might be swallowed.

- Keep portable heaters and heat registers protected from baby's reach.

- Keep house plants away from baby's reach. (Refer to Month 10 for a listing of poisonous plants.)

The 7-Month-Old

Free to Roam

Provide baby with plenty of open space for scooting and creeping. Keeping baby in the playpen for long periods can inhibit his or her growth and development. Baby gains knowledge and self-confidence as he or she is given the freedom to roam and explore. Be sure that baby's open space is supervised and blocked off from potential hazards.

Picking Up

During mealtime, place several O-shaped pieces of cereal on baby's highchair tray. Encourage baby to pick them up.

Meeting Strangers

Hold baby in your arms when someone who baby does not know or recognize approaches. Greet the person and talk to baby about the new acquaintance. This will help your child feel more secure and comfortable when meeting new people.

Side to Side

Show baby a favorite toy. Place it next to him or her. Encourage baby to turn to one side to find and get the toy. Place the toy on the other side of baby. Baby will be motivated to turn in the other direction to retrieve the toy. Finally, have baby watch as you place the toy behind him or her. Does baby know to turn around to get the toy?

Covered Up

Play peekaboo by covering your face with a towel. Ask "Where's Mommy/Daddy?" See if baby pulls at the towel to find you.

Tug and Pull

Tie an elastic cord around a rattle. Have baby hold the rattle. Gently pull on the cord. Baby will feel the resistance and will learn to hold onto the rattle. This helps strengthen baby's grasp.

Practice Makes Perfect

Continue to imitate baby's vocalizations. Baby will be motivated to repeat sounds, which are the building blocks to verbal communication.

Reel It In

Attach a long elastic band to each side of baby's highchair tray. Tie a small toy or a rattle to the end of each band. Place the toys on baby's tray. Show baby how to drop the objects and retrieve them by pulling up the bands. This activity will occupy baby while you are busy preparing meals. Remove elastic cords from the highchair when baby is creeping on the floor. This prevents baby from pulling down on them.

Find Me

Hide behind a chair or another piece of furniture close to baby. Call out baby's name and encourage him or her to find you. Continue talking until baby creeps toward you. Act surprised when you are discovered. Give baby a hug and kiss for finding you.

Funnel Fun

Introduce funnels and measuring cups as water toys during bath time. Show baby how cups are used to scoop and pour water. Pour water from the funnel over baby's body parts as you name them.

Grab and Pull

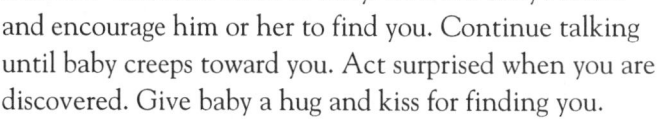

Tie a small toy onto one end of a 24- to 36-inch-long ribbon. Show baby how to retrieve the toy by pulling the ribbon toward you. Straighten the ribbon and this time encourage baby to get the toy. Let baby play with the toy a few minutes before repeating the activity.

Busy Box

Attach a busy box to one side of baby's crib or playpen. Baby will delight in the sounds he or she creates by pushing, pulling, squeezing, and hitting.

This Old Man

This old man, he played one.

He played nick-nack on my thumb

With a nick-nack-paddy-whack,

Give a dog a bone.

This old man came rolling home.

Additional verses: he played two/ on my shoe;
he played three/ on my knee; he played four/
on my door; he played five/ on my hive; he
played six/ on my sticks; he played seven/ up
to heaven; he played eight/ on my gate; he
played nine/ on my spine; he played ten/
once again.

Traditional

Language is listening and understanding as well as speaking. It is the foundation for later learning. The first four years of a child's life are the peak years for learning language.

Be Prepared

Situations or emergencies may arise that would require you or a babysitter to seek help to ensure baby's safety or well-being. Be prepared for such emergencies by keeping a list of telephone numbers near your telephone. Be sure to include the following:

- Police department
- Fire department
- Emergency "911" or its equivalent
- Ambulance service
- Poison control center
- Location of parents, if out
- Baby's pediatrician
- Parent support group
- Close friends or relatives

Toys and Playthings for 7- to 12-Month-Olds

- busy box
- cardboard or cloth picture books with large, brightly colored pictures
- tub toys (rubber animals, boats, sponges, funnels, cups)
- push and pull toys
- dolls, stuffed animals
- nesting toys (boxes, cups, and so on)
- stacking rings
- non-breakable mirror
- wooden blocks
- drum
- xylophone
- soft blocks
- pots, pans, and boxes with lids
- canning jar rings
- simple puzzles, with one or two knobbed pieces
- cymbals
- puppets
- large ball
- vehicles with wheels

Ring Around the Rosie

Ring around the rosie,

A pocketful of posies.

Ashes, ashes,

We all fall down.

While holding your child, turn in circles. On the last line, sit down.

Traditional

The 8-Month-Old

Tissue Box Book

Place colorful pictures on all six sides of a cube-shaped tissue box. Cover the box with clear self-stick paper. As baby tips the cube, new pictures appear.

Out and In

Set out a box containing several of baby's toys. Show baby how to take the toys out of the box. Then encourage baby to help you put the toys back into the box.

Follow the Sound
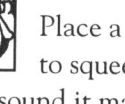
Place a squeak toy behind your back. Continue to squeeze it so that baby can find it by listening to the sound it makes.

Homemade Drum

Use an empty round oatmeal container as a drum. Show baby how to bang on the drum with a wooden spoon. Praise baby for the sounds he or she makes.

Let's Dance

While playing a favorite song, lift baby to a standing position. Encourage baby to bounce and dance to the music as you continue to hold his or her hands.

Ring-A-Ling
Hold a bell by its handle and show baby how to ring it. Give baby another bell. Encourage baby to ring his or her bell along with you as you sing the song "Ring Your Bell," on the page below.

Rolling Book

Turn a large round oatmeal container into a book for baby. Glue bright pictures on the outside of the box. Then cover the box with clear self-stick paper. Baby will love rolling the box and seeing all the pretty pictures.

Practicing
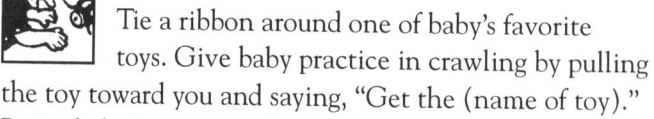
Tie a ribbon around one of baby's favorite toys. Give baby practice in crawling by pulling the toy toward you and saying, "Get the (name of toy)." Praise baby for getting the toy.

Flight of the Bumblebee
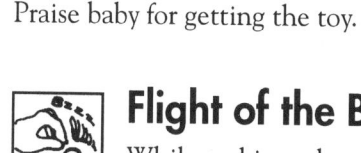
While making a buzzing sound, purse your fingers together to represent a bee. Make the "bee" fly around baby as you recite the rhyme "Bumblebee, Bumblebee" on the page below. Make your bee fly slowly enough so that baby can keep track of it with his or her eyes.

Rings and Things

Place several metal canning jar rings in a shoebox. Put the lid on the box. Shake the box. Encourage baby to retrieve the rings by lifting the lid off the box.

The Chase

Get on your hands and knees and crawl toward baby. Exclaim, "I'm going to catch you!" Play a game of chase with baby. Baby will squeal with delight as the two of you crawl after each other.

Paper Bag Puppet
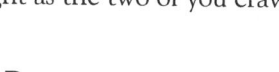
Place a small paper bag flat on a table with the flap at the top. Use felt tip markers to draw a face on the flap. Use the puppet to talk to baby. He or she will enjoy the crinkling sound that the bag makes when you use your hand to lift and lower the flap as the puppet talks.

We All Fall Down
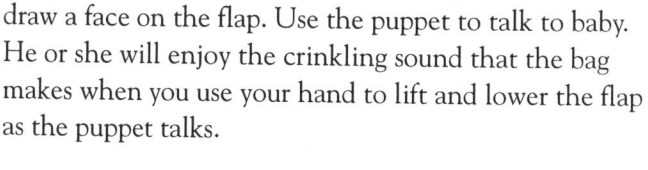

Hold baby in your arms. Walk in a circle around the room as you sing the song "Ring Around the Rosie." Sit down in a chair when you get to the line "We all fall down." Baby will enjoy the up-and-down movement.

I Love You

Sung to: *"Skip to My Lou"*

I love you, yes I do,
I love you, yes I do,
I love you, yes I do,
Here's a kiss that's just for you!

Kathleen Cubley

Baby's Teeth

Baby's first primary tooth will most likely be a lower front tooth. This will occur between the age of 6 to 10 months. Baby will have two to four teeth by his or her first birthday. By the age of 3, all 20 of baby's primary teeth will have emerged. Although they will eventually be replaced by permanent teeth, it is very important that proper care be given to baby's primary teeth. Baby relies on them for chewing and learning to speak. The following tips on dental care can help promote healthy teeth and a healthy smile for your baby.

- Do not put baby down for a nap with a bottle. Any unswallowed milk or other liquid (besides water) pools around baby's teeth and causes tooth decay.
- Avoid feeding baby drinks and foods that have a high sugar content. Sugar causes tooth decay.
- As soon as baby's first tooth appears, use a clean, wet washcloth or a piece of wet gauze to gently clean the tooth at least once a day. Continue this practice as more teeth emerge.

Bumblebee, Bumblebee

Bumblebee, bumblebee,
Buzzing all around.
Bumblebee, bumblebee,
Buzzing on the ground.

Bumblebee, bumblebee,
Buzzing up so high.
Bumblebee, bumblebee,
Buzzing in the sky.

Bumblebee, bumblebee,
Buzzing past your toes.
Bumblebee, bumblebee
Buzzing on your nose.
(Touch baby's nose.)

Jean Warren

Playtime should be a happy time. Use a variety of facial expressions, voice patterns, and hand gestures as you play with baby.

Ring Your Bell

Sung to: *"If You're Happy and You Know It"*

Ring your bell in the air, in the air.
Ring your bell in the air, in the air.
Ring your bell in the air,
For you haven't got a care.
Ring your bell in the air, in the air.

Jean Warren

Metallic Melody

Join baby in dropping wooden blocks into a large, empty metal pan. Baby will delight in the sound made by the blocks hitting the metal surface. Empty the metal container and encourage baby to repeat the activity. (Be sure the pan has no sharp edges.)

Clap and Click

Have fun with baby as you clap hands, wave, click tongues, and smack lips while singing the song "They're a Part of Me" on the page below. Encourage baby to imitate your actions.

Outdoor Explorer

Give baby opportunities to crawl through the grass. Talk about its color and how it feels and smells. Be sure to supervise baby when he or she plays outdoors. (Do not allow baby to crawl through grass that has been treated with chemicals.)

Velcro Poster

Sew several 2-inch pieces of Velcro onto an 18-by-24-inch piece of heavy canvas cloth. Sew the matching pieces of Velcro onto small cloth objects such as a sock, a mitten, a doll, a 3-inch-square carpet sample, or a washcloth. Attach these objects to the cloth poster by pressing the Velcro pieces together. Hang the poster on the wall near the floor. Show baby how to pull off each object. Reattach the items to the chart. Baby will enjoy pulling them off again and listening to the sound made by the Velcro when it separates.

Going to the Mall

Take a trip to the shopping mall. Describe to baby the various specialty shops: "This is a shoe store. Let's go inside and find a pair of shoes for Mommy." "Look at all the cards in the card shop. Help me find a birthday card for Grandma." Be sure to point out interesting people and things as you walk through the stores.

Obstacles

Place pillows on the floor to create an obstacle course. Show baby how to climb over and crawl around the pillows.

A Lovely Sight

Place a non-breakable mirror near the floor. Baby will be motivated to crawl to the mirror to look at his or her reflection.

Egg in a Cup

Assemble the halves of 12 brightly colored plastic eggs. Secure the halves of each egg with tape or glue. Encourage baby to place each egg in an opening of a muffin tin. Name the color of each egg as it is placed in the tin. Empty the tin and repeat the activity.

Putting on Socks

Dressing time can be a perfect time for baby to listen to and enjoy the wonderful sounds of language. Sing songs and simple nursery rhymes as you dress baby. Sing the song, "Let's Put on Our Socks," on the page below, while putting on baby's socks.

Baby's Space

Give baby his or her own dresser drawer to open and close and to fill with and empty of favorite toys. You can also set aside a kitchen cabinet with pots, pans, and lids for baby to empty and play with.

Baby's Picture Book

Cut out several bright, colorful pictures from magazines. Glue each picture onto a 5 ½-inch by 8-inch piece of cardboard. Cover both sides of each cardboard page with clear self-stick paper. Punch a hole at the top and bottom left-hand corner of each page. String the pages together with elastic cord. Baby will enjoy looking at the pictures and turning the

Safety on the Move

In a short time, your baby will be "on the loose" as he or she masters the ability to walk. Now more than ever you must take every precaution and make every effort to child-proof your home.

- Be sure that patio and other external doors are locked to prevent baby from roaming outside.

- Baby is intrigued with drawers and cabinets. He or she will reach for medicines, cleaning products, knives, and scissors. Make sure these items are stored in a secure place and out of baby's reach.

- Keep the handles of pots and pans turned inward on your stove, table, and countertops. This prevents baby from pulling down on them and receiving injuries.

- Slightly open windows should have guards to prevent baby from opening them any further.

- Supervise baby's outdoor activities. This helps prevent your child from swallowing a mushroom, a flower, or a plant that can make baby extremely ill or even cause death. Refer to Month 10 for a list of poisonous plants.

Little Boy Blue

Little boy blue,
Come blow your horn.
The sheep's in the meadow,
The cow's in the corn.
But where is the boy
Who looks after the sheep?
He's under a haystack,
Fast asleep.

Traditional

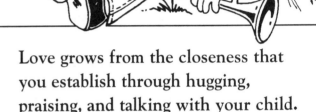

Love grows from the closeness that you establish through hugging, praising, and talking with your child.

Let's Put on Our Socks

Sung to: *"Hickory, Dickory, Dock"*

Hickory, dickory, dock,
Let's put on our socks.
We'll walk around
Without a sound
When we put on our socks.

Jean Warren

They're a Part of Me

Sung to: *"The Wheels on the Bus"*

I can make my hands go clap, clap, clap,
Clap, clap, clap,
Clap, clap, clap.
I can make my hands go clap, clap, clap.
They're a part of me.

Additional verses: I can make my tongue go click; lips go kiss; hands go bye.

Frank Dally

Blowing Kisses

Encourage baby to imitate your actions. Spread your arms apart and say, "(Baby's name) is this big!" Then say, "Blow Mommy a kiss!" as you show baby how to do it. Other actions baby can imitate include waving, clapping hands, and stirring with a spoon.

Road Trip

A ride in the car can provide baby with many learning experiences. Point to and name interesting objects, vehicles, people, and animals as you pass them. Talk about *stop* and *go* as you start and stop the car. You can also pass the time listening to music, reciting rhymes, or singing songs such as "I See a _____ Outside," on the page below.

Hello?

Make pretend ringing sounds. Encourage baby to pick up the receiver of a toy telephone. Make vocalizations that he or she can imitate while on the phone.

Loving Touch

Baby loves the feel of your touch. Walk your fingers up and down baby's arm as you recite nursery rhymes and sing songs. Move baby's hand up and down your arm, too.

Block Drop

Set a small shoebox and a bowl of blocks next to baby and encourage him or her to drop the blocks one at a time into the box. Help baby dump the contents on the floor. Clap at baby's accomplishments.

Stacking Rings

Show baby how to place and remove the plastic rings of a stacking toy that has a flat base. The flat base prevents the toy from rocking back and forth while baby is trying to manipulate the rings.

Bedtime Story

Before bedtime, spend two or three minutes reading to baby. The soft tone of your voice relaxes your child and helps him or her associate reading with a warm, pleasurable experience.

Sing and Sway

Hold baby's hands while he or she is standing. Begin singing a song and swaying back and forth with baby. Move baby's hands and turn him or her around. Don't forget to shake your head. Encourage baby to imitate your actions.

Nice Puppy

Babies often inadvertently treat pets too roughly. To show baby how to pet a dog or cat, show baby a stuffed toy animal. Say "softly, softly" as you and baby softly pat and stroke the fur. Encourage baby to softly pet other stuffed animals.

Circle Puppet

Cut a 3½-inch circle from cardboard. Draw a smiling face on one side of the shape. Cut two 1-inch holes near the bottom of the face. Place your index and middle fingers through the holes. Have the puppet ask baby to point to different parts of his or her body. Reward baby by using your fingers to walk the puppet to the body part and tickle it.

Musical Recital

Show baby how to press the keys of a toy piano or bang on pots and pans with wooden spoons. Provide lots of applause.

Choo-Choo

Place an empty cardboard box upside down on the floor. Encourage baby to stand up and push the box around the room. The box offers the support needed to help build baby's confidence while learning to walk.

Poisonous Plants

Babies and young children are attracted to the colors, textures, and smells of flowers and plants. Their curiosity often prompts them to eat vegetation that can make them very ill or even cause death. It is important, therefore, that you teach your child to never put plants in his or her mouth. To help prevent accidental poisoning, keep household plants out of baby's reach. To reduce the chance of poisoning from plants outdoors, supervise baby very carefully when he or she is outside.

More than 700 plants in the United States have been identified as poisonous. A partial list of the more common ones is listed at right. Please call your local Poison Control Center for a more complete list or if you think your child has eaten a potentially harmful plant. (Never assume that plants or berries are non-poisonous because birds eat them.)

Autumn Crocus	Holly	Morning Glory
Azalea	Horse Chestnut	Mushrooms
Belladonna	Hyacinth	Nightshade
Bittersweet	Hydrangea	Oak Tree
Bleeding Heart	Ivy	Oleander
Buttercup	Jack-in-the-Pulpit	Philodendron
Castorbean	Jasmine	Poinsettia
Cherry Tree	Jimson Weed	Pokeweed
Daffodil	Laurel	Poppies
Daphne	Lily-of-the-Valley	Potato leaves
Dieffenbachia	Lupine	Tomato vines
Foxglove	Mistletoe	Yew

Make a point of reading in front of your child. When he or she sees you reading, your child learns that reading is important.

I See a _____ Outside
Sung to: *"The Farmer in the Dell"*

I see a dog outside.
I see a dog outside.
Heigh-ho, away we go,
We're riding in the car.

Substitute other things you or your child may see outside for the word *dog*.

Jean Warren

Merry-Go-Round

Merry-go-round, merry-go-round,
We go riding all around.
First we're up, then we're down
    (*Move baby up and down on knee.*)
We go riding all around.

Merry-go-round, merry-go-round,
We go riding all around.
Hold on tight! Don't fall down!
    (*Lean baby slightly to one side.*)
We go riding all around.

Jean Warren

The 11-Month Old

Crumple and Rip

Show baby how to crumple a small piece of newspaper or wrapping paper. Encourage baby to imitate your actions. Then show baby how to tear the paper into pieces. He or she will enjoy doing this.

Dance, Turn, Clap

Take advantage of baby's enthusiasm for music. Help him or her dance, turn, and clap as you sing the song "Dance, Dance, Dance," on the page below.

Problem Solver

Place one of baby's toys in a paper lunch bag. Fold the open end of the bag closed. Encourage baby to open the bag and remove the toy.

Meaningful Sounds

Encourage baby to "tell" you what he or she wants when pointing to something. This gives baby practice in using sounds to communicate.

Over the Edge

Sit with baby at the table. Take turns pushing toy cars across the flat surface. Can you push hard enough to make the cars roll off the table?

Please and Thank You

Ask baby to hand things to you or to family members. Don't forget to say "please" and "thank you." By doing this, you model polite behavior for baby.

Puzzling Situation

Help baby assemble a puzzle that is made up of two or three pieces. Puzzle pieces with knobs are easier for baby to grasp and handle. Give lots of encouragement and assistance. Baby's skill and

Felt Book

To make a book, stitch a stack of felt squares together on the left-hand side. Cut simple shapes, such as a ball, a flower, a house, a star, a heart, and a car, out of felt. Glue them to the pages of the book. Encourage baby to feel the soft pages as you point to and name the objects in the book.

Nesting

Show baby how to nest a ¾-cup measuring cup into a 1-cup measuring cup. You can also demonstrate how a small plastic bowl fits into a larger one. Can baby do it? Give lots of praise.

Go Get It

Show baby one of his or her favorite toys. As baby watches, hide the toy somewhere in the room. Then say to baby, "Go get the (name of toy), please." Praise baby for his or her efforts in retrieving the toy.

Hand to Mouth

Allow baby to experiment feeding him or herself with a spoon. More food will probably wind up on the tray than in baby's mouth, but this is how children learn to eat. Praise baby's determination and efforts.

Scribbling

Cut open a large paper grocery bag. Tape it on the floor with the blank side up. Give baby a jumbo-size crayon to hold. Guide baby's hand on the paper to produce scribbles. Encourage baby to scribble without your help. Be sure to supervise this activity.

Ticking Away

Hide a ticking clock in a shoebox. Place the box near baby. Encourage baby to find it by

Dance, Dance, Dance

Sung to: *"Ten Little Indians"*

Dance, dance, dance, little Jesse,
Dance, dance, dance, little Jesse,
Dance, dance, dance, little Jesse
While we sing this song.

Turn, turn, turn, little Jesse,
Turn, turn, turn, little Jesse,
Turn, turn, turn, little Jesse
While we sing this song.

Clap, clap, clap, little Jesse,
Clap, clap, clap, little Jesse,
Clap, clap, clap, little Jesse
While we sing this song.

Substitute your baby's name for *Jesse*.

Jean Warren

Baby's First Shoes

Baby has been working very hard at learning to walk alone. Very soon, he or she will be able to walk with relative ease. You can help baby achieve this goal by allowing him or her to walk barefoot indoors as much as possible. Walking without shoes helps strengthen baby's foot muscles. As he or she masters the art of walking, or when walking outdoors, dress baby in shoes that are soft and flexible. Shoes with stiff uppers and soles can restrict baby's foot movements and make walking more difficult.

Celebrate Baby's Accomplishments

Baby's first year of life has been filled with wonderment and excitement. In a mere 12 months, your child has evolved from a tiny, helpless being to a curious tot who is busy exploring the environment and trying new experiences.

This is a time to celebrate your baby's accomplishments. He or she will continue to learn and build on past achievements with your constant support, love, and encouragement. Try not to compare baby's progress with that made by other children the same age, or even with your other children's development. Baby is unique and will develop at his or her own rate.

This is only the beginning of a long and adventurous journey for you and your child. Savor each moment as you provide experiences that help your baby learn and grow.

Diddle, Diddle Dumpling

Diddle, diddle dumpling, my son John
Went to bed with his trousers on.
One shoe off, and one shoe on,
Diddle, diddle dumpling, my son John.

Substitute your baby's name for *John*.

Traditional

Typical Developmental Behavior of Babies

The following lists represent typical behavior babies exhibit throughout their first year of life. Do not be alarmed if your baby does not exhibit all of the behaviors listed. Remember, each child develops at his or her own rate.

The 1-Month-Old:
- Stares at objects but will not reach for them
- Makes eye-to-eye contact
- Can roll partway to the side when placed on his or her back
- Thrusts arms and legs
- Lifts head momentarily while lying on his or her stomach
- May often move arms and legs without control in response to reflexes
- Turns eyes and head toward a light
- Grasps your finger
- Grasps a rattle but drops it immediately
- Becomes irritable or falls asleep when overstimulated
- Is aware of differences in textures
- Is startled by sudden, loud noises

The Newborn:
- Keeps hands fisted
- Jerks body in response to reflexive impulses
- Sleeps 16 to 18 hours of the day
- Can best see objects that are between 8 to 10 inches away
- Cannot yet distinguish colors
- Blinks at a bright light
- Responds more to soft, higher-pitched voices of women rather than to lower-pitched men's voices
- Can distinguish mother's voice from voices of other women
- Prefers the human voice to other sounds
- Relaxes to soft singing, humming, and gentle rocking
- Will suck when inner part of lip is touched

The 2-Month-Old:
- Bats at objects
- Enjoys watching three-dimensional objects
- Makes sucking motions with the mouth at the sight of a bottle or a breast
- Smiles at faces
- Uses eyes to track an object going from side to side, up and down, or in a circular path
- Coos, sighs, and grunts
- Visually recognizes parents
- Prefers to look at moving objects rather than stationary ones
- Lifts head with greater ease
- Sucks on objects
- Is beginning to have voluntary control over body movements
- Holds a rattle briefly before dropping it
- Is soothed by the sound of a familiar voice

The 3-Month-Old:
- Enjoys looking at picture books with an adult
- Puts things in his or her mouth
- Pushes out with feet when held in a standing position
- Loosens clenched hands; hands are more open and relaxed
- Uses facial expressions to communicate
- Holds up head and leans on elbows while lying on stomach
- Spends a lot of time inspecting the movements of his or her hands
- Uses eyes to search for sound
- Can hold and wave a rattle for a few seconds
- Grasps things voluntarily
- Responds to voices by cooing and gurgling
- Sleeps between 13 and 15 hours a day

The 4-Month-Old:
- Rolls over
- Enjoys using legs for kicking, flexing, and swimming motions
- Looks at rattle in hand
- Can see colors
- Recognizes familiar faces
- Rolls from side to stomach to other side
- Drools a great deal and may show signs of teething
- Naps two to three times during the day
- Laughs out loud, shrieks, and chuckles
- Calmed by soothing music
- Shows interest at sight of toy
- Loves to smile
- Turns head toward sound of bell or rattle
- Is alert for longer periods of time
- Can focus on objects at a

The 5-Month-Old:
- Can sit propped up for 10 to 15 minutes
- Explores objects by looking, holding, touching, and tasting
- Transfers objects from one hand to the other
- Communicates with smiles and vocalizations
- Scoots on stomach by kicking legs or rocks on all fours
- Turns from back to stomach
- Smiles at image in mirror
- Likes to bounce in jumper
- Will follow sounds in a darkened room
- Stops crying when he or she hears a parent's voice
- While lying on stomach, extends arms and legs
- Picks up spoon
- Plays with toys that can be pulled, grasped, or hit

The 6-Month-Old:
- Lifts head when lying on back
- May sit up unassisted
- Stands while holding onto something or someone
- Bangs objects
- Giggles, squeals, grunts, or screams to express feelings
- Is wary of strangers
- Uses voice and body movements to attract attention
- Enjoys playing peekaboo
- Lifts a cup
- Reaches for objects and puts them in mouth
- Manipulates food by biting, chewing, sucking, crumbling
- Examines others' faces by pulling hair, grabbing ears, poking fingers in mouths, noses, and eyes
- Turns from side to side to look around while sitting
- When hands are held, tries

The 7-Month-Old:
- Creeps by using arms and legs to pull body forward
- May scoot backward
- Sucks on own toes
- May hold bottle
- May show hand preference
- Recognizes parents' voices coming from another room
- Begins to respond to own name
- May have one or two teeth
- Grasps a rattle and shakes it
- Protests and resists doing something undesirable such as giving up a toy
- May fear strangers
- Has greater concentration when examining details of objects
- Begins to use fingers to grasp fingerfoods
- Attempts to imitate speech sounds
- Pats and smiles at own image in a mirror
- Vocalizes sounds such as *ma, mu, da, di*

The 8-Month-Old:
- Stands momentarily when hands are held
- Can hold an object in each hand
- Crawls on hands and knees
- Begins to grasp small objects with thumb and forefinger
- Pulls him or herself to a sitting position
- Uncovers toy when playing a "hiding" game
- May fear strangers, new situations, and places
- May fear separation from parents
- Says "da-da" and "ma-ma" indiscriminately
- Loves to babble
- Enjoys games such as throwing toys off highchair, peekaboo, and horsey
- May take one or two naps a day
- Enjoys listening to talk and rhymes
- Looks at objects that you point out

The 9-Month-Old:
- Understands the meanings of names of objects, as well as familiar people
- Crawls while holding an object in one hand
- Bangs two objects together
- Places lids on pots and pans
- Crawls up steps but cannot get down
- Understands and responds to simple directions
- Enjoys playing a game of being chased and caught
- Opens cabinets and drawers and empties contents
- Repeats own sounds and babbles in strings
- Puts objects in cups or containers
- Stiffens body when annoyed
- Continues the need to be in the same room as mother
- Holds bottle to feed self
- Tries to imitate sounds made by another person (cough, smack lips, click tongue)
- May fear loud noises

The 10-Month-Old:
- Sits, stands, turns, changes position, and crawls
- May cooperate during dressing
- Sways and bounces to rhythmic music
- Shows preferences for foods, people, and toys
- Looks at pictures in books
- Imitates gestures, facial expressions, and vocalizations
- Points to simple body parts
- Enjoys pull toys
- Uses specific sound for an object (*ba* for bottle)
- Stands alone momentarily
- Removes object from cup
- Displays happiness, anger, sadness, stubbornness
- Overturns items
- May walk while both hands are held
- Drinks from a cup that is held by someone
- Throws toys and expects others to return them
- Pokes fingers in holes

The 11-Month-Old:
- Attempts to take a step without support
- Loves to open, close, empty, bang, and throw objects
- Stoops and squats
- Drinks from a cup
- Points to familiar objects when hearing their names
- Shakes head to indicate *no*
- Puts spoon to mouth
- Hands toy to an adult
- Fills and dumps containers
- Attempts to scribble
- Likes nesting toys
- Cruises while holding onto furniture
- Enjoys taking objects apart
- Remembers where specific toys or objects are stored
- Squeezes squeak toys
- Pushes toy car
- Begins to turn pages of books
- Lowers self from standing position to sitting position with relative ease
- Enjoys rolling ball

Totline® Fun

●

Just for Babies

Let your children experience the wonder of learning
with hands-on activity ideas

Totline Books

TEACHING HOUSE SERIES

These books introduce parents to the everyday opportunities for helping young children learn with the teaching tools found all around the house and everywhere they go. Easy-to-follow directions for using ordinary materials combine family fun with learning. Teach your child about language, art, science, math, problem-solving, self-esteem and more!

Perfect for parents

Teaching House
ISBN 1-57029-068-7 • WPH 2801

Teaching Town
ISBN 1-57029-069-5 • WPH 2802

Teaching Trips
ISBN 1-57029-070-9 • WPH 2803

For use with children ages 2–5

Each book has 128 pages

Helpful illustrations!

PIGGYBACK® SONGS

New songs sung to the tunes of childhood favorites. No music to read! Easy for adults and children. Chorded for guitar or autoharp.

Piggyback Songs
A seasonal collection of more than 100 original, easy-to-sing songs for children! 64 pp.
ISBN 0-911019-01-4 • WPH 0201

Eleven books in the series!

Practical parenting advice

A YEAR OF FUN SERIES

Designed to hang on a wall, each book is filled with age-appropriate activities, games, recipes, and songs for every month of the year.

Just for Babies
ISBN 1-57029-049-0 • WPH 2701

Just for Ones
ISBN 1-57029-050-4 • WPH 2702

Just for Twos
ISBN 1-57029-051-2 • WPH 2703

Just for Threes
ISBN 1-57029-046-6 • WPH 2704

Just for Fours
ISBN 1-57029-047-4 • WPH 2705

Just for Fives

We wish to thank the following teachers, childcare workers, and parents for contributing some of the ideas in this book: Karen Brown, Dry Ridge, KY; Frank Dally, Ankeny, IA; Ann M. O'Connell, Coaldale, PA; Betty Silkunas, Lansdale, PA.

Editorial Staff

    Editor: Kathleen Cubley

    Contributing Editors: Gayle Bittinger, Jean Warren

    Copy Editor: Kris Fulsaas

    Proofreader: Mae Rhodes

    Editorial Assistant: Kate Ffolliott

Design and Production Staff

    Art Mangager: Jill Lustig

    Book Design: Susan Dahlman

    Book Layout: Sarah Ness

    Cover Design: Brenda Mann Harrison, Susan Dahlman

    Digital Coloring: Sarah Ness

    Cover Illustration: Susan Dahlman

    Production Manager: Jo Anna Brock

ISBN 1-57029-049-0

Printed in the United States of America
Published by: Frank Schaffer Publications, Inc.
                d.b.a. Warren Publishing House

Editorial Office: P.O. Box 2250
                     Everett, WA 98203

Business Office: 23740 Hawthorne Blvd.
                     Torrance, CA 90505

20 19 18 17 16 15 14 13 12 11 10 9 8 7